A STRANGER'S MUSINGS

COLLECTION OF SELF-ARTICULATED POEMS

SOURAV KUMAR SAW

Made with ♥ on the Notion Press Platform
www.notionpress.com

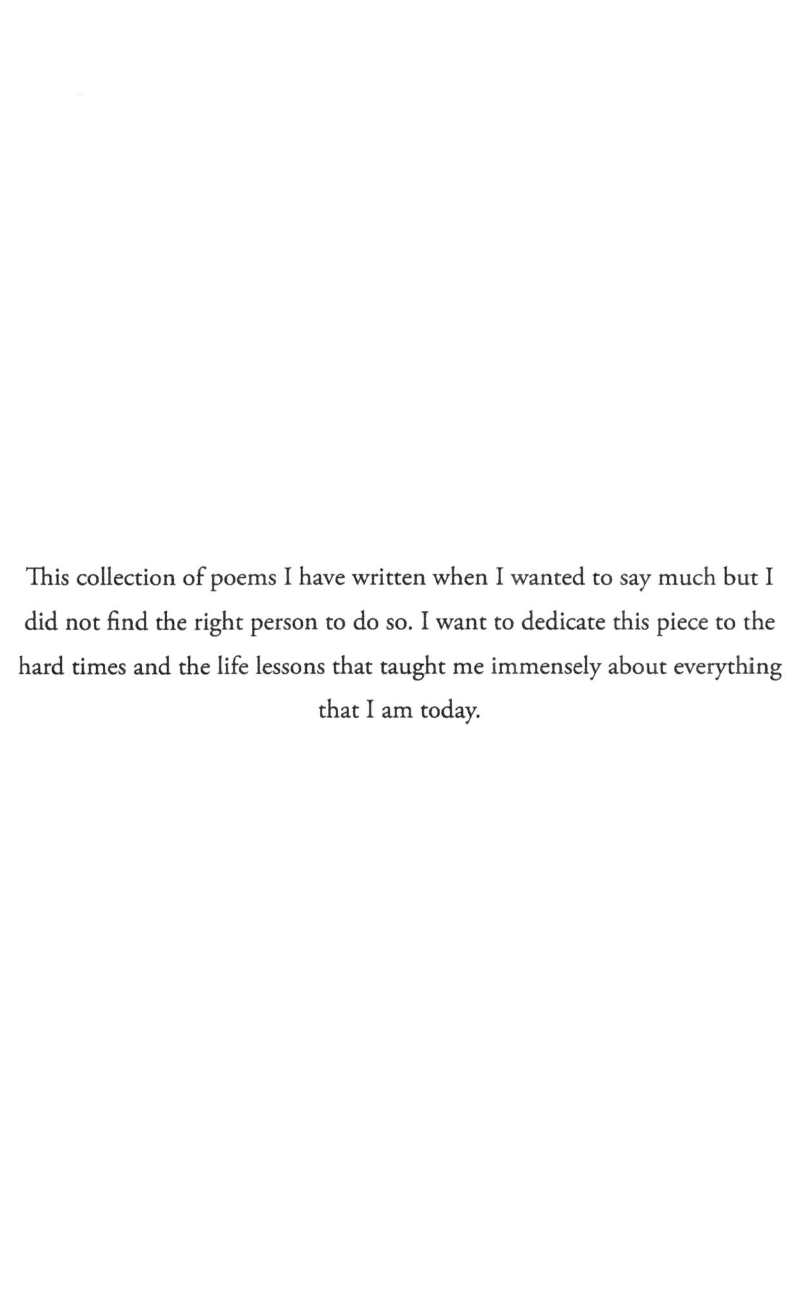

This collection of poems I have written when I wanted to say much but I did not find the right person to do so. I want to dedicate this piece to the hard times and the life lessons that taught me immensely about everything that I am today.

Contents

Preface

To everyone who still have faith in poetry, and who chose to feel than to think I offer this A stranger's Musings to you all to have a drink of this alcoholic poems and enjoy every bit of it. I wish I can touch readers heart with this.

Acknowledgements

To those whom I love- I owe them this book. I also want to shower my respect to my readers who will find this collection as an amazing gift to them, that they can cherish for a very long time.

You either live or you leave.

1. Rooh

I sat beside the lake where we first met,
when we were teenagers, full of vigor and
zest. You were with your friends making
paper boat and trying to float it away but
in vain. Everytime it sank. I came to your
rescue, made the boat again with few
variations and it floated. I still laugh
at the spooky look you gave to me.
I blinked at you and asked your name.
But you didn't say a word. Like obvious
I made frequent visits to that lake
and to my coincidence I kept finding
you. We grew closer and soon begin
dating and strangely, two strangers
became lovers out of nowhere. I don't
know if you remember, the dahlia bouquet
I gave on your nineteenth birthday? I
surmise, you might! We were scared to
be separated even for a day. Like the
bees to honey.
Ahh, how things toppled upside
down? Just a fraction of time. The
face we adore the most, are the ones now
that we hate the most. You betrayed my
love. You changed me. You spoiled me.

I wish now you to be a dream. To get over.

2. Asharfiyan

Touching you felt like a miracle,
like a heavenly bath into the Ganges
purifying soul and gratifying cognizance.
There's an ocean of emotion into
your eyes, that you never disclosed
before. I would want to delve deep into it
and find the lost pearl that you were
hiding beneath it. A marvel in itself.
Your mascara resembled rustling
leaves of Gulmohar, tiny and delicate
creating a pattern of diverse intricacies,
difficult to comprehend but easy to
lost in. Your lips sparkled that
tenderness of beauty, ready to be
kissed and felt how beautiful it could
be. Nevertheless, you wriggled
your fingers over my cheeks, like
the Juliet who found her Romeo, ready
to held him in that deadly silent night.
I closed my eyes. To feel it again, the love
of yours. I wish you could be here, again,
wiping my tears, kissing my cheeks,
and whispering, I have finally come to
meet you, my love. You are gone.
So does our love.

3. The last memory

I have a letter to write
which has long been
pending to get inked
with emotions flowing
through my body. It's
waiting for your name
to get etched in it, like
the daffodils you wear
back in your hair. The
ink wants to get
consumed describing
the piousness of your
soul. It wants to be
the testimony of how
rare you were. It feels
really tough addressing
you in every minute
details. An embodiment
of everything. I remember
when I started over,
I crumbled it. How
can anyone comprehend
this?
The ambience
intensified with lightening.

It is an indication
that I should stop. The
lights went off. I put
on the candle and stared
at it . I could see you, there,
waving me the final
goodbye. Might be
You were surreal. Might
be us too.

4. Heart Ache

These days my eyes don't long
for a face to stare at. My body
is worn out with the potion of
love at every phase of my life.
Love is not in my life, I am not
destined to be with some one,
I guess so. Never ever I had
chance to love some one to
the fullest. Is it my fault that
I encounter love at the most
feeble and meek point of my
life when things were falling
apart? I know there may be
people who strive and make
it happen. Maybe if I try to
explain anyone, they'll
say the same. But they won't
understand the pain and struggle
I go through, every single day.
Try to be in my shoes for a day
You won't even consider falling
in love, rather you won't think
of love itself.
I am going through a tough
test in my life. The test of

life. I understand now, love is just vague concept which doesn't last long. It never will. The decision and commitment will. I guess, in my case I never will be able to do so. Now music is my ultimate companion. I listen to it and think of the times I spent with you. Maybe for small time. Still I cherish it. I remember someone asked me- Can lovers be friends again? I didn't answer then. Because it's pointless. You only truly love for the first time. Rest is the role you play to be a lover, which you actually aren't.

5. Gila Shikwa

The silence between us is
consuming me every single
day. Do you remember,
how we used to chit-chat
the whole day, even the whole
night about the silly things
that made no sense? Still
we liked what we did? Every
single time we played
with words to make each other
laugh. We were there for each
other's to cry upon. I don't find
all these now. I guess things are
starting to fade. Maybe our love
too. We don't express anymore.
About anything. About our work.
And above all, our love. We don't
show gestures to flirt with each
other. We don't even fight
over silly talks, anymore. I guess
we are in such phase of love,
which is vulnerable. Do you
remember when was the last
time we talked about us?
I believe, Love and light

eventually dim, when not
taken care of at the right
place and right time.
I don't know what future beholds
for us. Maybe we'll come to know
about all, shortly. You know there's
always a strange silence before the
storm. I guess this is such storm.
Adios!

6. Judaaiyan

No, I never stopped loving
you. Ever wondered why I
paused when you asked me
why I stopped talking to
you? You words pierced my
body deeper than the dagger,
recently sharpened
on the wetstone. Maybe you
won't believe the circumstances
I was tormented with. I know
it was hard for you too. To
continue without me, to move
past without holding my hand.
I cried every night
thinking about you. About us.
Every dawn, nature painted the
sky with the color of your
mascara, and every dusk it
faded. Every day I woke up
remembering your face. It hurt
me to eternity. There's a thing
about love, it's an endless
ocean which tests human
who dives into it. It demands
sacrifice. It demands to let

go.
My body has become a
jigsaw puzzle, with you
missing to complete it. Every
word I pen down clicks your
essence in my mind. I miss
the very comfort of holding you
in my arms, dancing and
gazing into you eyes. Some
seconds have really become
a time maze that I am still
stuck on. I want to relive
the moments with you
again. I hope to see you
soon.
Miss you

7. Gehraiyaan

The darkness of the forest
made a silhouette that
resembled you. The hustling
leaves felt like your hair
waving and calling me
by my name. The eeriness
of silence that's spread
everywhere, impaired me.
Like the firefly, that's
been abstained to glow.
The cold chilly wind
rushed through my body,
petrifying my spine. The
stars made a pattern
to proclaim the inevitability
of oblivion. I went in, your
silhouette faded and
gloominess prevailed. All
of a sudden, cold breeze
grazed though my ears
and whispered-"this emptiness
is a testimony of betrayal".
Heavy heartedly, I
kept going inside
the dark forest and lost

myself in your silhouette.

8. Gumrah

I saw a moth at the dusk
pondering alone, lost track
of his path. It went north,
then suddenly changed its
path and went east. Again
after a much turmoil, it changed
its path. It took west.
The direction of sunset. Perhaps,
it was direction-less, still
it trusted its instinct, with
a scattered beam
of hope to find its lost home.
Nobody knew, it was right
direction or not, still it chose
to move ahead. It gave
me goosebumps on the
thought of how a tiny creature
could be so tough in its hard
times. It's determination to
keep moving, gave me a tight
punch on my face. I thought
of quitting and that my life
had no purpose left. My
everyday seemed out of
meaning. My pillow even

pitied me everyday hiding
my teary eyes within it. I
was blank about my life and
where it was heading to.
I was left alone.
Someone said good things
take time. No person has
ever achieved greatness,
without facing hard times.
It's my turn now. There's
always a silence before
a tsunami. I guess, this
is the same.
Hey, I won't give up.

9. Lamhein

I breathe.
Only to release out the
remnant of our memories.
It cringes me. My soul.
I abstain from daisy
flowers now, because
it hurts when its aroma
hits my nostrils
that recreates the time,
you sent me a bouquet
of those to surprise
me on my birthday.
I still have the picture of
us. I keep staring at
them , even though my
eyes hurts to the extreme.
Those flashbacks blur
my vision. I miss the
feeling of us being
close to each other,
holding hands and
making promises to
never let go.
Do you remember
how we romanced

on the song-"Love me
like you do"?and
evening turned to night?
I hope, you do remember.
Every beautiful journey
has an ending. For us
too. We loved, fought, cried
but just like every good
thing, it ended. Abruptly.
Nevertheless, we had
a memory to cherish
for lifetime.
Don't we?

10. Khoya aasmaan

I still remember, how beautifully
you caressed me when I got a
cut on my forearm. You tore apart
your beautiful dress to heal my
injury. You silently cried, and those
warm teary pearls fall over my wound.
It was warm. A symbolic of how your
heart was crying out in grief. You
prepared coffee for us. I deliberately
dropped my cup, for us to share
the single one. You sipped, then I.
It continued. With watery eyes you
kissed on my cheeks, and joyfully
we went to the terrace. We lay
our heads close to each other,
watching the stars as it
shimmer all across the sky. We held
hands and promised to never leave. Just
like the paper boat which we happily
put on the water to sail but just like every
happy story, it ended. It sank. Today,
I prepared a coffee but it
lacked the flavor.
I tried adding more coffee beans
and sugar but it already lost the

most important ingredient. It lost you.
It lacked your essence. I went to
terrace to witness the stars. It
didn't feel the same. It felt gloomy.
I understood it the hard way
that it's arduous to find the people
who would walk by your side
till the end of life. Isn't it?

11. Darmiyan

It's hard to love someone
when you are hollow
from within. Every word
echoes in your ears
like the ripples, that
the sliding pebble creates
in stagnant water, fading
and vanishing ultimately.
It's really hard to
comprehend anything
furthermore. Just like
the aging man, who's
seen everything and
many more, your heart
becomes a crescent
moon, more vulnerable
than the shame-plant
that wriggles in with a
slight touch. It is afraid
to witness storm. Once again.
Still, you do it. You love.
Don't you?
Can loving someone be
ever enough?

12. Saansein

My heart's a mess. It has
always been. The strings
were tangled and rugged.
The dust of emptiness
made it hard to symphonize
with the aura of romance
spread everywhere. Good
music urged it to untangle,
and transform to the kind
of art it was meant for. It
utters in silence, to fall in
love again, and witness
the silhouette, the genre
it had always waited for. My
eyes blur when my favourite
song plays, reminding me
how we could have been
wild and carefree.
I still remember, how I
surprised you with fresh
jasmine flowers, and you
hurriedly attached it to
the back of your hair.
I know, it's withered.
You too. All seasons feel

alike now. Rain doesn't
excite me now, rather, it
brings back the reminiscences.
Of you. Of us.
My heart's a mess. It will always
be.

13. Dooriyan

It's 3 AM, and I stare
at the sky hoping to hunt
your face out of it.
I know this quest is
meaningless, but the
twinkling of stars reminds
me of you. I can sense your
presence everywhere. Amidst
the murmuring cold breeze, I
hear your tranquil whisper, as if
it's craving to perceive me.
Faraway, there's a lone star that
resembles your eyes, glaring
it's prestige everywhere. The
rustling leaves is crooning
"saude baazi" song to haggle
you with the distance separating
us. Now, Anuv Jain songs hurt
even more and winter feels
colder and unforgiving. It's
hard to stay away from
someone you admire and
adore the most. It becomes
harder when you are blank and
vacant about when you'll

see the love of your
life, again. I wish we had
telepathy power. Alas! it's
surreal. Honey, close your eyes
and feel me. Feel us. I am
present in every bit of you.
Honey, let's keep on creating
such beautiful moments, in and out,
throughout. Remember not to
forget to cherish the memory
for life time. Okay?
It's 3:30 AM, and I miss you, darling.

14. Ek ishq aisa bhi

Was that for real when
you texted back? Did you
still love me after all the
chaos? I never knew you
would become an integral
part of mine. Wasn't that
strange, how love kept us
bound even if there seemed
meager probability of us to
fall for each other. You kept
the thread intact, and tried
every possibility, to proclaim
how much I mean to you.
Still an stranger, you trusted
me and with your vision of
love and desire, we finally met.
I am still dazzled, how you
eavesdropped my steps
and came out to surprise
me. Is it some kind of super
natural phenomenon that
I am still unaware of? I
couldn't believe how anyone
can love someone so deeply!
Did you develop an invisible

force to wrap me in its aura
of piousness? Didn't you fear
a bit, how I would be as a
person? How could you trust
me so blindly? It was a surreal
feeling for me. I never knew
life kept a jackpot round
for me to witness. A round, that
would change the course of my
destiny. I always stared at
the moon when I felt low in
my life, but you came out to
be a blue moon waiting for me
since eternity. Did you know, it
was so comforting when you
hugged me? It felt like I
achieved everything in life.
The warmth of your body
comforted me and I could
hear our heart beat
synchronizing, teleporting
us to a land of fairy tale, where
everything seemed possible and
in our possession. Our love
was not just love. It still isn't!
You touched that part of mine
that I was always scared to
share with anyone. You saw me,
when no one else did. You looked

into my eyes. I saw an entire
universe over there. Honey, the
way you held my hand was way
more ballistic, and the way you
kissed, felt like an tsunami of
emotions, wriggling all over my
body. Your tender touch created
a nursery of blooming flowers, which
once was left barren to die.
Honey, let's close our eyes and feel
each other's breath, and live the
moment as we always wanted.
I know, you have scars. You have
never been loved the way you
wanted with the people you believed
in. Still, you fought everyday to
sustain and create a name for you.
I know, it's not easy. You have an
untold saga to utter. You fear.
We all do. Honey, I have come to
heal each broken part of yours.
You have endured a lot, beyond
your limits. Hey, I want to hold your
hand and walk this path of life
together, and create a golden
chapter in the book of my life.
I want to immortalize you. Every
bit of you. I want the world to
know how amazing and beautiful

you are. Honey, you have already
become the protagonist of
my novel.
Hey, I miss you
|| Grow while you row through the storm ||

15. The rising flamingo

The kind of touch you grant
is admirable. I know, I am unknown
to the scars you are begotten
with, still I know, you are bestowed
with a destiny, you can't escape.
I am a broken guy, with a crumbled
heart. You made me alive with
the painting you drew on my
hand. The bird, the unchained
falcon willing to fly high
ripping off the sky, reaching
the top most where godliness
and holiness fail to make
sense. I wonder if we ever
get the chance to
love each other. It won't be
just us, but the greater prominent
force which the almighty could
never imagine. I can trace the
entire milky way to find your
presence. You revived me
from the ocean I was once
lost in. I know it's tough
for you too. Our paths are
diverged and our astrology

speaks differently but I know,
we will create a abode, where
the hatred will be engulfed with
love, darkness will be
overpowered by mystic lullaby,
sung by the creators of this
unrealistic world. I wish, people
knew it's not for them to adore
the enchantingly superficial abyss
where there is nothing but hell. Just
like the moths that flew in the
evening and vanish. I hope, our
lives will be dedicated to
something more beautiful,
something more pious where
we can proclaim peace and
allow the world to love. I hope
to remember you like the shakura
cherry blossom, whose every
withered petal speaks an
unsaid story, that's
engraved in my
heart. Forever. Hey stranger,
you gave me an
amazing memory, which I am
gonna cherish forever.
Adios.

16. Unknown Silence

When words fail to
make sense and you
realise, you have
been overpowered by
an invisible
accoutre of darkness,
which you have no
control of, you sing
a hymn to yourself,
trying to stop the tears
from stepping down
your lids. You move
to the mirror and
watch it wriggle down
your cheeks,
slowly outreaching
the chin.
They are scared to
fall and part with your
body, but that's how
the law of nature
works. They drip.
Separate. With blurry
eyes, I saw it fall
into the dust, a land

where ultimately
everyone find their
home after
death. You silently
open your favorite book
and read your favorite
lines in it. You feel
its pangs. That's what
we as writers
go through.

17. The frowzy twilight

I stood there
numb watching
you as you stared
at him. My eyelids
froze on that very
moment and I could
hear the rain drops
spearing arrows
right through
my heart. My
eyesight blurred
and I dropped
my cell phone
impassively. Cracked.
It carved a rugged
boundary on your
saved picture in my
gallery. The
thunderstorm
escalated the plot
more viciously,
and lightening
gave the
final climax. You
kissed him. With teary

eyes I picked up
the phone, wiped
out my tears. I left
the scarf. There. The
one you gave me,
and promised to
never leave me.
Drenched in rain, I
looked back to
get your last
glimpse. Honey,
our forever is
now over.

18. Atoot Rishta

You said, you had
your supper even
though it's been days
since you had a proper
meal.You said, you
had bought the
dress recently even
though, it's been
years you have got
a new one.
You said, you had a
proper sleep of
8hrs but it's been
months you slept
properly. You said, you
just wanted to marry
and raise a family
but deep down, you
have forsaken
your ambitions and
dreams. You said you
do not want to
continue job although,
it was the one which
you were once

ready to die for. I know,
how unwillingly you
parted with it. For the
people you love. To
nourish them into a
good human being.
You said you left
painting because
it doesn't interest
you anymore but
who knew you
gave up your passion,
for us to
follow ours. You
always wanted to
fly high like a
falcon. Unfortunately,
you gave into circumstances.
For us.
For the people
you love. You have
learnt to hide your
emotions so well,
that you cry deep inside
but smile from outside.
My first love, you were
the person whom I saw
for the first time, I came
to the world.

It's strange, even the goddesses
get something in return
if the offerors wishes
are fulfilled. Why don't
you? Why society
has created
such a disparity?
Mother, you are
beyond
everything. Incomprehensible.
Hey mother,
I love you.
To the moon and back.

19. Phases

Ever felt so hopeless in life
that you lay on bed for
days and still feel tired
about anything and everything?
Nothing interests you anymore
and you become the iron toy
that's been rusted without
being touched for months.
Breathing feels tough to take
and you consider yourself
becoming burden on every
body. You lose your long
harvested hobby and even
picking the paper gives you
heartache. Remembering how
time changes with the choices
you make, gets you ponder
over the things that could
have been right. Nevertheless,
it's pointless now. If ever I
revive and find someone
who will show me light
I won't leave that person.
Ever.

20. Breakthrough

Will I succeed now? Will my
terminal loop come to an end?
Will I be set free from the
endless loneliness? My heart
fears about the consequences
that may change the course
of my journey. My path,
altogether. Its difficult,
but that circle of
rejections soon found
a loop-hole. For me.
To make my
way out of that darkness.
I want my life to be big
and different. I don't want
to die being normal. I want
the world to remember be
as a crazy lad who broke the
shackles of desolation to
fly high into the sky. Soar
through the top most clouds,
making a living example for
anyone who wants to do so.
No matter how hard we're
crushed, we should have

the courage to get back
to our feet and show
the world what we are
capable of. The day will
reckon soon when I'll
rise with flying colours.
To my surprise-
" The day has come"

I cannot express how hard it has been for me to miss each aspect of you. You left me with an incurable void. You made me what I was always scared of.

9 798888 838273

Printed by Libri Plureos GmbH in Hamburg,
Germany